# YOGA

# YOGA

## The Oriental Healing

NAVODITA PANDE-BHARGAVA

PARTRIDGE

A Penguin Random House Company

**To order additional copies of this book, contact**
Partridge India
000 800 10062 62
orders.india@partridgepublishing.com

www.partridgepublishing.com/india

# Dedication

For My Guru

My parents and the Chanchanis

# Comments

'I didn't think Yoga could be such a rejuvenating exercise until I learnt it from Navodita'

Swati Bhattacharya, Psychology student, New York University

'I loved doing Yoga and saw Navodita bend her body in artistic styles and thought it was mesmerizing to look at her doing Yoga like that'

Deborah Wolk, Yoga practitioner, Iyengar Yoga Institute of New York

'Yoga energizes the body and makes it feel agile, active and hungry for more. This feeling did not come to me until I started doing Iyengar Yoga with Navodita'

Students of Cardiff Yoga Studio, Cardiff

'I started doing Yoga only recently when Navodita introduced me to the subject and I haven't left it ever since. This is a wonderful workout for the body, mind and for distressing.'

Aizey Jaffri, Management student, Cardiff University

'I only knew Yoga as a word. I was introduced to it by Navodita and learnt all the basics from taking off your shoes to learning the basic shoulder-stand. It's been wonderful.'

Anchal Berry, Employee, Meyhar Bhasin Grooming Academy, New Delhi.

'I needed some asanas for my ovarian cyst and needed somebody's help. I turned to Navodita and low and behold I felt better with those prescriptive asanas.'

Ashrita Shukla, Lecturer, Jagran Institute of Management & Mass Communication-Kanpur

# Contents

Foreword........................................................................11

Acknowledgements........................................................13

Introduction..................................................................15

Preface..........................................................................19

**Section I**

**Yoga and Body**...........................................................23

> ➤ Yoga for Body ......................................................24
> ➤ Yoga for Eyes........................................................27
> ➤ Yoga and Chakras ................................................29

**Section II**

**Yoga and Mind**...........................................................31

> ➤ Yoga for Depression ............................................32
> ➤ Yoga for Schizophrenia........................................35
> ➤ Yoga for Autism ..................................................37

**Section III**

**Yoga and Spirit**..........................................................39

> ➤ Yoga and Breath..................................................40
> ➤ Yoga and Meditation...........................................42

**Section IV**

**Yoga and Therapy** ........................................................45

- ➢ Yoga for Spondilitis.............................................46
- ➢ Yoga for Indigestion ...........................................49

**Section V**

**Yoga and Living** ...........................................................51

- ➢ Yoga is a Way of Life...........................................52
- ➢ Easy Yoga workout for kids ................................54
- ➢ Yoga for Menstruation .......................................57

**Section VI**

**Yoga and Philosophy** ...................................................75

- ➢ Hatha Yoga Pradipika ........................................79
- ➢ Chanting with Faith............................................98

# Foreword

This is a good handbook for those initiating themselves into Yoga and wanting to know what Yoga is all about. Yoga is much deeper than what the word truly denotes, which is harmony. Complete harmony of the body, mind and soul is Yoga. It is rare to find a book which truly sums up Yoga as a lifestyle. This book is highly systematic and shows her expertise on the subject. She has mastered the art well while teaching it to youngsters and the elderly alike. It is commendable the effort she has made to bridge the gap between practical and theory of Yoga. Certainly it is a valuable tool for young practitioners of Yoga.

I believe that in Yoga simply theory is not enough and practicing Yoga alone is not enough either. Its best effects can be achieved once complete harmony has been achieved in life.

Navodita has particularly taken care to identify such aspects within Yoga and chapterize the book accordingly. The last section on Yoga and life's philosophy is equally good. She has used several mantras and excerpts from the Bhagvad Gita which is indeed very useful to any young practitioner. Readers will find that the book easily explains the most difficult aspects in an easy manner.

This is a matter of immense pleasure and pride for me that Navodita is writing a book on Yoga. Truly Yoga is expertise in action or 'Yoga Karmasu Kaushalam'. That alone is the true definition of Yoga which has been well brought out in this book.

Mahant Shri Surendra Nathji 'Avadhoot'
Kalka Devi Temple,
Nehru Place
New Delhi

# Acknowledgements

Thanks first of all to Partridge Publications for accepting my proposal to publish this book on Yoga. I thank Joe Anderson for coordinating the publication of this book on behalf of Partridge Publications. It is thanks to Partridge that I got inspired to send some of my pictures in the Yoga poses which adds to the content of the book. Without the time and inclination of Partridge Publication, the book would have been impossible. I thank them for letting me flout deadlines and giving me my freedom to complete the book at my own pace and leisure. I must also thank my mother, Rekha Pande, for inspiring me to publish this work on Yoga. I have been doing Yoga as a child but it was thanks to the constant encouragement and support of my mother in particular I carried it along with me uptil here. I also thank my father for initiating me into Yoga as a child which has culminated into this book today.

If they helped me in bringing out this book, the origins of the book go back further when I began learning Yoga from various sources. I am sure I have absorbed things from professionals in the field of Yoga when I was learning it at Dev Antarrashtriya Yoga Kendra in Kanpur with my father's friend, Dr. Om Prakash 'Anand'. I must thank Swati and Rajiv Chanchani for teaching me Yoga as a child and giving me the opportunity to start teaching at the young age of sixteen in school. It gave me the confidence required to move ahead in Yoga. I also thank Guruji B.K.S. Iyengar for his unflinching faith in me when I went to RIMYI for training in Pune. His words 'If you do yoga, Light on Yoga will shine in you', still make me feel proud of my Yoga practice as a child. I thank Hare Rama Hare Krishna Mandir, New York for giving me a chance to teach Yoga. I thank Cardiff Yoga Studio, Meyhar Bhasin Grooming Academy for giving me a chance to teach it to young people. I also thank New Delhi Television Limited (NDTV) for telecasting my Yoga show on television and giving me an appropriate slot both on English channel, NDTV 24x7 and on Hindi channel, NDTV India. I must thank my mentors at Iyengar Yoga Institute of New York, Mary Dunn and Brooke Myers for teaching me Yoga for a brief period.

Alongside, I have learnt Yoga at Shivananda Yoga Ashram and in the Art of Living course which has constantly added to my resource base of knowledge about the field.and have probably contributed in some way to the ideas within this book. Even talking about meditation and Yoga to the Buddhist nuns and monks at Dharamshala, McLeodganj helped. It was all contributory to this learning process. I trained the nuns in Yoga giving them notes in the Tibetan language which also somewhere contributed to the knowledge base. The contents of this book have also been informed by discussions with my Yoga students in various places- it helped me in understanding the needs of the reader and the one starting off in Yoga. *Yoga: The Oriental Philosophy* would not have been the same without the help of Mahant Shru Surendra Nath Avadhoot of Kalkaji Temple in New Delhi. I owe this to my roots grounded in Hinduism although my students have come from diverse backgrounds.

The finished book owes much to you all, although responsibility for any errors and omissions rests with me.

# Introduction

Yoga is a way of life. I realized this early in life at the age of five when my father first taught me to bend myself into a Pashchimottanasana and stand erect in a Shoulder Stand. Little did I realize that this was to help me for the rest of my life.

I took up Yoga as a co-curricular activity in boarding school at Welham Girls' School at the age of nine. That is when Rajiv and Swati Chanchani, disciples of Shri B.K.S. Iyengar began training us in Iyengar Yoga. I loved to do Yoga as a child and I preferred doing it more as a physical exercise than anything else. As I grew up my Yoga practice continued and I represented my school in several national and international Yoga demonstrations. I gave a lecture-cum-demonstration at International Yoga Week in Rishikesh, too, along with a bunch of my classmates from The Doon School.

There was a time when I started bunking Games Time in school to do Yoga. Then my Yoga practice also made me bunk prep in school even though my Board examination was coming closer. While everybody would sit in classrooms finishing their homework, I would be busy bending, twisting and stretching in Yoga with a few other handful of Yoga enthusiasts. I never loved my life more with me doing Yoga for almost four hours a day. At the age of fifteen only, I was selected along with nine other girls to represent school and get trained at the Ramamani Iyengar Memorial

Yoga Institute in Pune which was established by Shri B.K.S. Iyengar.

The routine at RIMYI was amazing. All of us slept in a dormitory-style hall of beds in an ashram run by Catholic sisters called C.P.S. Ashram or Christa Prem Sewa Ashram. We had a rouser at 5 a.m. everyday and left for the Institute at 5:30 a.m. to reach there by 6. It was a lovely walk through the lush and green Agricultural Institute o Pune. We were all instructed to drink some jaggery water before the class so we remain energized throughout. Jaggery water was always kept in one corner of the dining hall where we sat on the floor and ate food.

After a rigorous Yoga workout of two hours at RIMYI, we socialized and chatted a little with other international Yoga practitioners there, talked to the administration staff and left for the ashram to eat breakfast. The food we got here was specially prepared for us for fifteen days. It was kept strictly Sattvic and without any spices which spice up the senses. Our breakfast would be two loaves of brown bread, a boiled vegetable or sprouts, white clarified butter, lots of fruit and a glass of milk. We all got together in the dining hall, sat around on the mats and ate food while sitting on the floor. Breakfast was followed by some essential Sewa. Sewa meant cleaning the area which we were assigned. Each student was assigned an area that she had to clean. I got toilets on the first day, library the second day and bedrooms the next day and so on. The morning cleanliness went on for about two hours after which we all were expected to spend some time reading in the library. I usually chose a book on Iyengar and his life. We sat reading till 12:30 p.m. It was now time for lunch. Lunch, too, was had a specially prepared menu for us. Lunch usually had one seasonal dry vegetable, lentils, chapattis and brown rice. This was followed by a fruit. We were supposed to have a siesta after lunch. Some people would continue their reading, etc. This would be rejuvenating time for the next Yoga session from 5 p.m. to 7 p.m.

After the evening Yoga class at 5, we would again walk back to the ashram, shower and get changed to sit for a hearty dinner. Dinner was again a vegetable curry with brown rice and chapattis. After dinner we followed our pastime and chatted and slept.

It was a lovely trip of fifteen days. Later I was to come back again to RIMYI and C.P.S. Ashram to stay here for fifteen days to relive the memories. This time I was older, independent, mature and an adult. I stayed here, did Sewa as per the rules of the Ashram and had a wonderful time that I was to always cherish. I also taught yoga to Fathers of different churches and chapels across the country who met here for a training at C.P.S. Ashram. I also attended the morning Sunday mass regularly for these fifteen days again.

I continued to teach Yoga during my graduation to women and kids in my locality in Allahabad. I taught therapeutic Yoga and instructed people in three years of my graduation. It was a very fulfilling experience to know from people that their back pain had subsided or their spondilitis pain had gone. I continued to teach Yoga when I was away in New York on a holiday for six months. I learnt at Iyengar Yoga Institute, New York and was teaching at Hare Rama Hare Krishna Mandir in New York. I also taught Yoga while I was working with NDTV. I used to teach Yoga to students of Meyhar Bhasin Grooming Academy, a finishing school in New Delhi. It is a wonderful experience to interact with younger students with lot of energy and enthusiasm.

I continued teaching Yoga while I was at Cardiff during my postgraduation. Cardiff Yoga Studio was a hub of young students willing to learn the art. I also taught Yoga at Kanpur while teaching at Jagran Institute of Management and Mass Communication- Kanpur to a few students and faculty members.

Yoga has been an enriching experience. While I did it for exercises in the beginning, as a kind of workout, it developed into my spiritual and emotional support over the years. Today Yoga is a way of life and a practice one needs to adopt. My practice of Yoga is closely related to my being a practicing Hindu. Yet Hinduism and Yoga are not the same, for me these two things have been interwoven. My chanting, fasts during Navratra festival twice a year, fasts every Friday for Vaibhav Lakshmi occasion, meditation and pranayama help me in being the holistic person I am. Hindutva or Hinduism is an offshoot. Yoga is a wider concept.

I wish all the readers a very pleasant reading. Please email me your feedback at navoditapande@gmail.com or post your comment on my blog www.navoditapande.blogspot.com

Enjoy the book!

# Preface

Yoga is an ancient science, art and philosophy. Lord Shiva is considered to have originated Yoga. Yoga is considered to be the precursor to many other forms of physical sport and games- gymnastics, martial arts, etc. It is said that Lord Shiva passed his knowledge of yoga to his consort, Goddess Parvati who then passed on this knowledge to the great sages. Sage Patanjali is considered to be one of the first great yogis. His work on Yoga called *Yoga Sutras of Patanjali* is very famous. *Yoga Sutras of Patanjali* has served as a key text for many other yoga books.

In this book the focus is on Yoga as one of the major ways of healing in the Oriental systems of wellness, fitness and rejuvenation. It is said that even cancer patients, when treated with some yoga asanas recuperate faster than those who only survive on medication and recover slowly.

Hatha Yoga is a form of exercise where each body part is focussed upon and activated by the flexible performing of poses or asanas.

Acuyoga combines a set of asanas keeping in mind the pressure points that will be pressed when recommending an asana for the practitioner.

Reiki is another divine form of exercising your body consciously by focussing on the seven different chakras or energy points in your body.

The Art of Living is yet another form of meditation and practice in which the focus is on the breath or pranayama.

Chanting mantras or positive lines is a very powerful way of recuperating or staying rejuvenated for the day. This, too, has been discussed in detail, and some important chanting mantras are provided in this book.

The purpose of the book is to provide the reader with a compendium of knowledge about different forms of Yoga and alternate remedies which can be used even while some form of medication or treatment is going on through any other form of medicine- allopathy, homoeopathy or Unani or even Ayurveda.

This book is, therefore, divided into six sections. Section I deals with different kinds of Yoga, the human anatomy and its complexities and how Yoga affects health. It mentions the various types of Yoga practiced in India and the world since ancient times. Yoga is practiced in numerous different ways. It is a practice which has constantly been evolving with modern day Yoga practices even incorporating Power Yoga, Dynamic Yoga, Bikram Yoga and the like. Some contemporary practitioners even include Dance Yoga and Art Yoga. Yoga has thus seen an evolution of sorts with each proponent pitching in their quintessential technique to classical form of Yoga. In this chapter we discuss classical and contemporary Yoga forms. This section discusses in detail the human anatomy for a Yoga practititoner. One must perform Yoga depending upon their body type. It is exactly like a doctor prescribing medicines for a patient. In order to understand which asanas suit your body the best, a practititoner must understand the human body and its complexities. Depending upon the deficiency your body may have, certain asanas are performed. For example, if one has constipation, focus will be more on stomach-based asanas that will improve digestion. The same set of asanas may not be prescribed to all yoga practitioners. Hence there is no universal yoga workout for all body-types. Chapter 3 is about Yoga and its contribution to health.

Section II in this book is all about other forms which are being combined with yoga. This segment focuses on wellness as a subject. Wellness is all about holistic health and its importance. Holistic health includes not only physical well-being but also mental, spiritual, emotional health with an emphasis on adopting a healthy lifestyle.

Section III deals with Yoga as a spiritual subject. The great Yoga practitioner B.K.S. Iyengar says, 'Yoga is an art, science and philosophy'. It is discussed how Yoga is beneficial for the physical body, mind and wellness of the spirit. Asanas and its close connection with the human anatomy is talked about. This section discusses the uses of Yoga for the mind. There are lot of Yogic Pranayamas, Kriyas and meditation and Dhyana which are very soothing to the mind. Yoga is not just for the body or the mind but a way of life. If this is adopted well, Yoga can do wonders for your life.

Section IV deals with therapy. This section understands yoga more as a science. The scientific understanding of yoga-asanas makes it possible to use yoga for therapeutic purpose.

Yoga can work wonders when used as a therapy. It, therefore, focuses on the use of Yoga in improving your health.

Section V is a segment dedicated to Yoga, mainly Yoga for life. Yoga is a way of life and requires aa certain lifestyle. It is important to incorporate Yogic lifestyle to be able to get the full benefit of Yoga poses or asanas.

Section VI includes chapters on metaphysics of Yoga, chanting mantras and other positive words for getting full benefit of the Yogic poses. This is about the Bible of Yoga-Hatha Yoga Pradipika.

Hence this book is not only about Yoga but also about how you may use Yoga and other healing practices for a holistic healthy life. Therefore the name- The Oriental Healing. Unlike Western systems of medicine, some good Oriental healing techniques believe in doing away with a disease completely by destroying its symptoms and slowly healing from within. Allopathy may provide you with a good medicine as an antidote but healing systems like Reiki, Acupressure, Yoga and exercises work within your body to make it internally strong to be able to fight a disease.

# Section I

# YOGA AND BODY

## Yoga for Body

Teaching yoga for over two decades has not been very tough. A challenging task, however, has been suiting it to different type of an audience or class. If the yoga class comprises kids upto the age of 12, asanas definitely cannot focus on each specific body part. The asanas will have to be simple, straight and introductory. On the other hand if the practititoner has been doing yoga for several years and has gotten used to bending and stretching, the asanas can remain focused on a particular joint or a muscle for several minutes together. It is understanding these minute details that are important while teaching yoga.

For example in a yoga class for senior citizens aged 60-65 years, one could incorporate simple standing poses which could work wonders in rejuvenating the body:

- Trikona Asana
- Vriksha Asana
- Garuda Asana
- Virabhadra Asana I
- Virabhadra Asana II

Similarly, a class for persons who are obese or leading a sedentary lifestyle wanting to take to yoga to shake that extra ounce of flab, a good yoga workout could have these asanas:

- Surya Namaskar
- Adhomukhasvana Asana
- Parsvakona Asana
- Jatara Parivartana
- Setubandha Asana
- Sarvanga Asana

On the other hand, for a regular practitioner doing yoga for at least five to six years a yoga session could be more intense with a focus on just standing poses, sitting poses, backbends or forward bends or even twisting, supine and inverted poses. There are more than 306 poses according to The Yoga Sutras of Patanjali, the famous Yoga treatise. The right permutation and combination could be used to suit the right student so by each yoga guru. Otherwise training can be a tedious task. So this is how a regimen can look for a regular practitioner:

| Week 1 | Week 2 | Week 3 | Week 4 |
| --- | --- | --- | --- |
| **Standing Poses** | **Sitting/ Twisting** | **Backbends** | **Inverted Poses** |
| Surya Namaskar | Paschimottana | Dhanur Asana | Sarvanga Asana |
| Adhomukhasvana Asana | Janusirsa Asana | Shalabh Asana | Viparitadanda Asana |
| Urdhvamukhasvana Asana | Bharadwaj Asana | Makar Asana | Hala Asana |
| Parivritta Trikona Asana | Ardha Matsyendra | Urdhvadhanur Asana | Sirsa Asana |
| Parivritta Parsvakona | Pasha Asana | Viparitadanda | |
| Parsvottana Asana | Kurma Asana | Rajkapota Asana | |
| Ardhachandra Asana | Kroncha Asana | Setubandha | |
| Virabhadra Asana III | Baddhakona Asana | | |

Hence each of these days, the asanas are practised for long duration, for four to five minutes at a stretch so that expertise can be gained in every posture. It is slowly and with gradual practice that one realizes that even the asanas are to be done according to one's body-type and according to one's stamina alone. After all the main end in Yoga is to achieve relaxation and calmness of the body and mind. Even over-stressing the body would be unwise. Ideal practitioner uses balance and poise to steer oneself to accomplish a healthy body.

## Yoga for Eyes

Come monsoon and with it the woes of catching an eye-flu. However if you regularly take care of your eyes, there are bleak chances of you catching an infection. Performing some good eye exercises is a must if you want, bright, clear, pretty large eyes. You could follow this eye-workout:

**Tratak or Gazing:** This system of gazing directly at an external object works wonders for strengthening the eyes. It is also a meditative technique where you have to keep a pointed finger in line with your eyes and stare at the tip of the finger. Meditate on it without getting distracted by external noise and thoughts. Harden your eyes and stare fixedly at the finger as though you are gouging eyes out in anger. Relax your eyes after repeated stares. Repeat this exercise and continue for about five to ten minutes.

**Eye-ball Movement:** Here there are several ways of performing the movement of the eye-balls which energizes the eye-muscles.

Begin by first moving your eye-balls from top to bottom. Look up and then down without batting you eyelids or without moving your head. Make sure only the eye movement is observed. Repeat the upward-downward movement of the eye-balls at least ten times.

Second method is to move your eye-balls from left to right and vice versa. Again ensure that you are sitting up and your back is straight. There should be no head movement. Repeat the side-to-side movement of the eye-balls at least ten times.

Third method is to move your eye-balls upwards, sideways, downwards and again to the other side. Make a full circle with your eyes. Perform this first in clockwise direction and then in anti-clockwise direction. Repeat this cycle at least four times in each direction.

One more way of exercising your eye-balls is by holding your right thumb slightly above the shoulder on the right-hand side and your left thumb slightly below (diagonally opposite to the right thumb) the shoulder on the left-hand side. Now stare at the tip of the right thumb and shift the gaze to the tip of the left thumb. Repeat this ten times. Perform the same movement with your left thumb raised up and right thumb below the shoulder. This oblique movement of the eye-ball strengthens the ciliary muscles.

**Sanmukhi Mudra:** Lastly here's something to relax the eyes after a strenuous workout for the eye-muscles. Shut your eyes and plug your ears with your thumbs and place your index finger gently between the eye-lid and the eyebrow. Your middle finger should be rested below the eyes, on the eyelashes. Ring finger is on the upper-lip while little finger is below the lips. Breathe deeply with the fingers gently touching the skin. Breathe deep for at least ten to twenty cycles.

Work on this routine for your eyes for about a month and continue to rejuvenate them every night before sleeping with cool cucumber slices on your closed eyes. You could even use two cotton swabs dipped in rosewater for making your eyes feel refreshed and protected against the changing weather, dust storms, snow and rain. Be sure not to touch your eyes with bare hands even to itch or twitch!

## Yoga and Chakras

Yoga, as we all know, is about harmony between the body, mind and soul. This harmony is achieved by various means- Yama, Niyama, Asanas, Pranayama, Pratyahara, Dharana, Dhyana and Samadhi. These eight wings or steps have been called the Eight-Fold Path or Ashtanga Yoga. Yoga works at one more level-that of meditation. Simply termed Dhyana, meditation implies full concentration and focus on various body parts. Ancient knowledge of the human body divides body energy into seven main chakras. Hence began the ancient meditative technique of focusing the mind on different chakras or energy channels in order to heal oneself mentally, emotionally and physically. Let's get a brief on the seven main chakras and their functions:

**Muladhar Chakra:** This Chakra is situated three fingers below the navel and is also called the 'Abdomen Chakra'. Here one needs to focus on the abdomen and adjoining areas to cleanse and heal oneself for ailments of the abdominal region and corresponding areas of the back; for example irregular menstrual cycle, abdominal pain, lower backache, etc.

**Swadhisthana Chakra:** This Chakra is located right beneath the navel and meditating on this Chakra heals the areas around the navel, stomach and corresponding areas of the back. Stomach ulcers, gastric problems, flatulence, acidity, diarrhea can easily be warded off by the right focus on the Swadhishthana Chakra.

Manipura Chakra: This Chakra is three fingers above the navel and below the rib cage at the hollow between the two lungs. Focusing the breath and mind on this Chakra relieves one of digestional problems and problems of the thoracic vertebrae.

**Anahata Chakra:** This is located at the centre of the body on the sternum (the breast-bone) between the two breasts. Focus on this area and you will find easy relief from pain and ailments of the heart, other coronary diseases, lungs and respiratory disorders like asthma, bronchitis, etc. This Chakra is also popularly called the 'Heart Chakra'.

Vishuddhi Chakra: Popularly called the 'Throat Chakra', mindful meditation on this Chakra is very helpful for throat problems, tonsillitis, goitre, speech disorders and stammering or lisping. Since this Chakra corresponds to the area of the oesophagus (food pipe) and the trachea (wind pipe), it is beneficial to work on this Chakra for easy passage of food and breath.

**Ajna Chakra:** This Chakra is situated a little above the eyebrows in the forehead. The Chakra is located between the eyebrows and energizing this means attracting a whole lot of focus, concentration and energy around this part of the brain.

**Sahasrara Chakra:** This Chakra is the imaginary energy point right above the crown of the head in line with all the other Chakras. Energizing this point is as good as rejuvenating all the Chakras and the central nervous system of the body.

A great and ideal meditative technique would be to stay on each Chakra for five to ten minutes. In all, you should take half-an-hour to complete the Chakra meditation. This meditation alone can help you get rid of psychosomatic illnesses, biological and medical problems with ease. Happy Chakra-ing!

# Section II

# YOGA AND MIND

## Yoga for Depression

Depression is something to do with a state of mind where the life is lacking an imbalance. For example, if one lacks a purpose in life, one can easily take to self-destructive habits of smoking, drinking or overeating, further weakening the physical and emotional state of being. The result is depression or negative state of mind with reduced sense of self-esteem and great loss of will power. How then can one redeem oneself from this through yoga? Do not be surprised. The key is to be mindful and open oneself to a sense of awareness and the guiding light that can change one's life. Here are a few poses to go out for when under mental duress.

### Learn About Alternate Nostril Breathing (Anuloma Pranayama) and Interrupted Brathing (Viloma Pranayama)

This form of breathing exercise or Pranayama is very beneficial for such a disorder or mental tension and stress. Here you need to sit comfortably in a simple cross-legged pose and breathe normally before starting with Anuloma-Viloma. Then slowly breathe in from one nostril and exhale from the other. Repeat inhalation from the same nostril for five minutes. Repeat with the inhalation from the opposite nostril. Do not rush the breathing. Continue slowly for five minutes, concentrating on the depth and rhythm of the breath.

### Downward Facing Dog (Adhomukhasvana Asana)

This pose works wonders for deep emotional stress. The psoe maybe done by placing the head on a blanket or by placing hands against the wall. Stay in this pose for at least five minutes.

## Down Face Tree Pose (Adhomukha Vriksha Asana)

This pose, too, is good for getting rid of mental stress and tension and any kind of mental block. Beginners of course must do this againt the support of the wall. Straighten the elbows. Pull the lungs in without letting the ribs protrude forward while in the inverted pose. Stay in the pose for five to ten counts. Repeat three times.

## Belly Turning Pose (Jatara Parivartana) – Bent Knees and Variation

This pose is ideally good for stomach problems and digestion but does wonders for emotional and mental troubles. When we are under stress frustrations creep in and weare not flowing with our feelings and needs but are pushing or resisting something in our life. The key is to drop the frustration, be able to step aside and observe and accept your frustration as part of a whole. This pose helps you do just that. Take the frustration headlong into your own hands and fight it.

So you lie on your back. Place your hands under your buttocks and bend your knees. Exhale and move your knees to one side towards the floor. Inhale as you centre you knees. Continue for one or two minutes, alternating sides. Relax on your back.

Revolved Belly Turning Pose (Parivritta Jatara Parivartana), too, is good where the knee of the reverse leg is brought down to touch the floor.

Idea is to release the stress and bring harmony and aliveness into your body movements.

# Yoga for Schizophrenia

Schizophrenia is a disorder characterized by lack of coordination between thought, words and deeds or actions. It is a psychotic ailment which medical practitioners say cannot be diagnosed completely. However, I believe, based on my work on schizophrenic patients that such persons have shown marked improvement in behavior with the practice of the following asanas and relevant community help, employment aid and family behavior therapy. Here's a look at how schizophrenics can best contribute to a healthy society by improving their social behavior with the practice of these poses:

**Dog pose I:** Adhomukhasvana Asana or the downward facing Dog Pose helps in is a great tool for curbing depression and anxiety disorder that comes with the disease. Inhale, raise your hands, exhale, bend forward, take two huge steps back, stretch your arms in front keeping your buttocks raised towards the ceiling. Rest the crown of your head on a stack of pillows or cushions if you cannot touch the floor. This posture helps regulate dopamine and serotonin release in the brain. Dopamine neurotransmitters are located in the deep middle region of your brain called the substantia nigra. The asana reaches out to the parts of the brain and is found effective in energizinging these nerve centres of pleasure and 'feel-good' sensation.

**Urdhvadhanura Asana:** This asana again helps to stimulate the brain cells responsible for social withdrawal symptoms, sloppiness of dress and hygiene, and loss of motivation and judgement found in a schizophrenic patient. Here you have to lie down on your back, place your arms taking them over the shoulder and placing the palms of your hand under the shoulder with elbows facing the ceiling. Bend your knees, exhale and push with your palms to raise your body against the floor. Ask your family member for help to raise your waist well-high up in the air. You could raise your heels off the floor. Stay in this pose for about sixteen counts. This is great for early diagnosis and reduce hallucinations, delusions and suicidal tendencies in advanced patients.

**Grasshopper Pose:** Shalabh Asana is great for again pushing your limits to work on your sense of paranoia, disorganized speech and thinking if you are a schizophrenic. Here you have to lie on your stomach, place your fist under your left groin, raise your left leg with thighs off the floor and chin on the floor, too. Then place your right fist under your right groin and lift the right leg off the floor. Lastly interlock your palms, place them under the inner thighs and lift both thighs off the floor together. Keep your legs straight as much as you can.

**Bhastrika Pranayama:** Sit up straight in Virasana or simply cross-legged pose. Place your hands rolled up in slightly-closed fists around your chest. Take a powerful deep breath in and raise your hands up in the air releasing your fingers and keeping them outstretched. Then exhale powerfully making a noise through your nostrils and bend your arms back to the original position near the chest. Repeat this cycle of Bhastrika Pranayama at least twenty times. Pranayam helps resolve the schizophrenic tendency of 'splitting of mental functions' in the body. It increases powerful blood supply to the brain and the heart, too.

Schizophrenia is again not incurable but a condition that can be overcome with the right conditioning and yoga therapy of the body. Perform the above asanas for a couple of weeks and notice the behavioural changes in the individual.

## Yoga for Autism

Autism is a neural condition which affects children usually around the age of three. It is characterized by social malfunctioning and repetitive behavior. Autistic people show signs of compulsive behavior, stereotypy, restrictive behavior and even self-injury. Such patients often suffer from misplaced communication; for example autistic kids may have a problem translating symbols into language and experience difficulty with imaginative play. Even among adults there are various symptoms that cannot be diagnosed by professional medical practitioners. Here's how Yoga can help tackle these problems in an autistic patient:

**Uttanasana:** This asana works wonders for autistic patients in regulating the blood flow to the affected parts of the brain. Asana may be performed by inhaling, raising your hands, exhaling and bending down to the floor. Make sure you don't push the person too much to bend further down towards the floor. The feet must be shoulder-distance from each other. The arms may be entwined or left loose.

**Pashchimottanasana:** It maybe difficult initially to motivate a patient to perform these asanas. Nevertheless once performed, Paschimottanasana is great for the brain stem, located in the front of the cerebellum in the brain. Increased flow and exercise of this part of the brain helps cure the maladjustment and disorderly communication in an autistic patient as brain stem is responsible for passing messages between the cerebral cortex and various parts of the body. Here you have to sit straight, raise your hands, exhale and bend over to try and touch your toes. Once again, don't try pushing too hard.

**Tortoise Pose and the Sleeping Tortoise:** These two poses, different versions of one and the same Kurma Asana, are very beneficial for activating the cerebellum, located at the back of the brain. In order to perform this asana, you have to first sit and spread your legs to leave enough space for your head in between. Bend your legs, slide your arms under the bent knees on either sides, and place your chin down on the floor. This asana helps improve motor activity, regulate balance and body movements in an autistic child. Improved communication, especially intrapersonal communication in a human-being may drastically show positive changes in the diseased person.

**Shoulder Balance:** This asana, too, works wonders for the brain's cerebellum structure as the back of the brain gets rejuvenated here. In this pose you are supposed to lie down on your back, bend your legs, place your hands on your back to support it and lift your body gradually off the floor, raising your legs up in the air. Ask for support of your family and friends to help you lift your legs in the air initially. Do this for about a minute. The patient will have improved speech and body coordination.

Practise these asanas daily for about fifteen minutes in all, supplement it with deep breaths in the end and you will notice milestone changes in the patient. Complement a good yoga routine with lots of social activity, community service and theatrical exercises. Autism is more of a condition that can be worked upon rather than treated with medical aid.

# Section III

# YOGA AND SPIRIT

## Yoga and Breath

Breath is the basic life force in a living being. Most students have appreciated the role of Yoga in controlling breath. Breath has a tremendous power to heal and to rejuvenate. Its importance in therapeutic cases cannot be undermined. Swami Ramdev has revolutionised the use of various breathing techniques or Pranayama all across North India. So, what are the different uses of breath?

According to Hatha Yoga Pradipika pranayama should be practised four times a day, in the early morning, evening and midnight, with 80 cycles at a time. The best seasons to practise pranayama are spring and autumn, when the climate is equable. Pranayama should be done in a clean airy place and preferably seated on the floor on a folded blanket. Suitable postures for that are Virasana, Padmasana and Baddhakonasana with an erect back and chin resting in the notch between the collar-bones and eyes lightly shut. So here are the various types of basic pranayama for starters:

### Nadi Shodhana Pranayama

Sodhana means purifying or cleansing, so the object of Nadi Shodhana Pranayama is the purification of the nerves. Perform Jnana Mudra with the left hand (index finger and thumb joined) and bend the right arm at the elbow. Bend the index and middle fingers and place them in the middle of your eyebrows. Press the ring and little finger against the left nostril while inhaling from the right and place the right thumb on the right side of the nose just below the nasal bone. Inhale through the left nostril, blocking the right one and slowly block the left nostril. Then release the right thumb and exhale through the right nostril, blocking the left nostril. Repeat 8 to 10 cycles. This should take about 6 to 8 minutes.

## Bhastrika Pranayama

Bhastrika means a bellows used in a furnace. Sitting in the same posture, follow this technique-Take a fast, vigorous breath and exhale forcefully with a loud sound of air gushing out of your nostrils. Complete 10 to 12 cycles at a stretch.

## Kapalabhati Pranayama

Kapala means skull and Bhati means light; this is a milder form of Bhastrika Pranayama. Inhale slowly but exhale vigorously. There is a split second of retention after each exhalation. Do a few cycles of Kapalabhati if Bhastrika feels strenuous.

## Benefits of Pranayama

While Bhastrika and Kapalabhati activate and invigorate the liver, spleen, pancreas and abdominal muscles; digestion is improved and sinuses are drained Nadi Shodhana is good for soothing the nerves. The real disclaimer here is that those suffering from high or low blood pressure, heart ailments or eye or ear complaints (pus in the ear, detachment of the retina) should avoid doing strenuous pranayama and perform 10 to 15 simple deep breathing cycles without holding the breath.

## Yoga and Meditation

Derived from the Sanskrit word 'Yuj' meaning to 'yoke' the mind, body and soul, Yoga and meditation works to build a certain harmony within the three aspects of the human body: physical, mental and emotional. A healthy body will have a perfect union of all these three aspects. One without the other will be incomplete or unhealthy. Therefore every illness or disorder means that healing is important not just at a physical level but also holistically at a subtle level, within the core of the body. In order that a person be cured completely, patient needs to get beyond the anatomy and heal the body within and heal the person within-emotionally and mentally, so that the healing takes place at a holistic level. It is for this reason that the inner strength is required to fight the disease and illness more than the curative poses or the workout.

Meditation proves to be a perfect addendum to such a workout. A workout in the morning could easily be followed by a meditation combination in the evening or vice versa. Meditation techniques build one's inner resolve, strengthen one's faculties to work towards one's goals relentlessly and with resolve. Concentration techniques help one focus on one's aim in life which is to pull oneself out of the negative state. One has to have the right frame of mind to get into the posture and sit in a simple cross-legged pose to be able to do a meditation and let negative thoughts find a way out and let positive thoughts walk in so that illness and disease can be gotten rid of.

## Sakshi Dhyan

This meditation technique is unique in that here the practitioner is only expected to sit with eyes closed, breathe normally with hands rested firmly on the knees, palms facing upwards. Breathe normally. Allow thoughts to come in and watch all sorts of ideas walk through your mind. Let the thoughts come and go. The idea of this meditation technique is to not let anything bottle up but flow out without causing anguish and a block. All you have to do is focus on your breath and your normal breathing pattern. Be a mindful observer. Sit in this posture for fifteen minutes. Rub your palms, prese the base of your palms gently against your eyes and open your eyes.

## Sanmukhi Mudra (Six-Headed Mudra)

This is a form of yoga posture that brings peace, tranquility and poise to the body and mind. Close your eyes. Place your index finger just below the eyebrow without pushing the eyeball. Place your middle finger gently pushing down the eyelashes. Place your ring finger on your nostril while the little finger is gently touching your upper lip. Plug your ears with your thumbs. Ensure that your fingers aregently touching the surface of your skin. Breathe softly, gently, slowly and deep. Perform the Bhramri Pranayama in this. While exhaling take out a hissing sound.

Gently relax and release your fingers. Lie down in Sava Asana. Feel the relaxation and the healing within.

# Section IV

# YOGA AND THERAPY

# Yoga for Spondilitis

It's common knowledge that when a particular body part stiffens it begins to develop into a sore. Tension develops, blood circulation is blocked and sedentary lifestyle can further aggravate matters. I had one such patient with a spondylitis in the neck. Spondylitis is an inflammation of the vertebra.

I came up with one good combo which I would make her do everyday for a month and it did wonders for her entire back. She claimed her spondilitis got a lot better. The idea was not to get into a quick workout but a slow recovery session where focus was on the body part. Taking deep long breaths in every posture paid dividends. Feeling the pose while staying in it and thinking that it is actually benefitting the body part helps in the process. Repeatedly thinking about your neck and your benefit from the pose actually makes you get a positive response from the exercise. So how to get started?

## Upward Facing Dog (Urdhavamukhasvana Asana) on 2 blocks

Place 2 blocks at a shoulder distance from each other, rest your hands on these with palms first facing towards your body. Stay in this pose for 10 seconds as the practitioner maybe a beginner. The head should be raised well, facing the ceiling.

Repeat this with the palms facing away from your body the other way. Stay in this again for 10 seconds. In both cases, head should be well raised facing the ceiling.

Repeat this with your chest touching the wall, hands rested on the blocks, palms facing the body. Stay in this pose for 10 seconds.

Lie down for 5 minutes and rest.

## Sitting Yoga Poses with head raised and a concave back

Seated Forward Bend (Paschimottanasana) with hands raised and head raised. Keep your chin stretched. Do not bend the head. Stay in the pose for 10 seconds.

Head-To-Knee (Janusirsa Asana) with head raised. Keep your chin stretched. Stay in the pose for 10 seconds on each side.

Half-Bound Lotus Intense Stretch (Ardha Baddha Padma Paschimottana Asana) with head raised and chin stretched out. Stay in the pose for 10 seconds each with either leg stretched out..

Three-Limbed Forward Bend (Triangamukha Eikapada Paschimottana Asana) with chin stretched and head raised. Stay in the pose for 10 seconds each with either leg stretched out.

## Twisting Yoga Poses with a Yoga Strap

Bharadvaja's Twist (Bharadwaj Asana) can be done simply where the neck must get a full turn. It should be done on both sides.

The Sage Twist (Marichya Asana) is good for the back and the neck but if it is done without bending forward. Simply sit straight, take your arm around the bent knee and use the strap and turn your head as much as you can. Stay in the turned position for 10 seconds. Repeat on the other side.

## Bridge Pose (Setubandha Asana)

Finally end by lying down and stacking up lots of blankets under the neck and shoulders. Let the head hang down on the floor. Rest in this with eyes closed for at least five minutes.

After first two weeks of this workout, backbends maybe added for a more intensive workout.

## Yoga for Indigestion

Modern lifestyle has a lot of demands on the body that can contribute to the problem of indigestion. Processed foods, chemically-treated, 'de-vitalized foods' such as artificially colored and preserved meats, dairy products, fruits, vegetables and products made with white flour or white sugar or both and eating heavy, oily, fried foods, rich sauces or desserts are often difficult to digest. Some common causes of indigestion can be emotional stress and tension, lack of exercise, overeating, wrong combination of foods or simply suffering from stomach ailments like constipation or Irritable Bowel Syndrome, etc.

There are some wonderful poses to rid oneself of these. These poses can be energizing. They rejuvenate the muscles, relax the body and ease the stomach of any tension. Restorative in action and curative in purpose, these poses are rather healing in nature. Here's to get started.

### Hero Pose (Virasana) and variations

The foremost asana to do for digestion and get your digestive juices working is this pose. This pose can be done even after eating or at any other time of the day. Those who need assistance may do this pose by sitting on a bolster or a cushion. Rest in this pose for five to ten minutes.

Reclined Hero Pose (Supta Virasana) is yet another good posture which maybe done after a meal. This again gets the digestion and metabolism started quickly. Support of bolsters and cushions maybe taken for the back while lying down in this pose. Rest in this posture for five to ten minutes.

## Supine Yoga Poses

These poses should be done on an empty stomach every morning or in the evening. The workout of supine poses may begin with the following asanas:

The Wind-releasing Pose (Pawanamukta Asana) where you bend your one knee and hold it with your hands and hold it down to your stomach. Exhale while you get your knee to your stomach. Press it down to your stomach keeping the other leg straight. Breathe normally. Repeat with the other leg. Repeat this five times. Repeat with both legs bent.

Upward Stretched Legs (Urdhva Prasarita Pada Asana) with one leg and a strap. Pull the raised leg towards the body. Repeat with the other leg. Repeat with both legs five times.

## The Bow Pose (Dhanurasana)

This pose is most beneficial for strengthening the nervous system and releasing body tension. It tones the abdominal muscles, helping to reduce abdominal flab and fat. It improves brain activity and affects most of the endocrine glands. It stimulates the thyroids, thymus, liver, kidneys, spleen and pancreas. Be sure to relax for more than five minutes after doing this strenuous and powerful backbend.

These poses mentioned above are like elixir for the tummy that can work to bring it back on a normal function and routine. The whole digestive system is restored and balance is attained.

# Section V

# YOGA AND LIVING

## Yoga is a Way of Life

An acrobat. An enchanter. Worse still, a magician – is what many people end up thinking about Yogis (practitioners of Yoga). Well, Maharshi Mahesh Yoga, Ma Nirmala Devi, Swami Shivanandji and Padma Vibhushan B.K.S. Iyengarji maybe called yogis par excellence but the real question is what exactly is Yoga?

Derived from the Sanskrit work "Yuj", Yoga means "to join". This implies communion of body, mind and soul; where Yoga, in other words, is the yoke. According to Oxford dictionary, 'yoke' is derived from the Old English 'gex' (ge=y), Latin 'jugum' and Greek 'zygon'. Yoga, literally, in itself is an abstraction. It denotes harmony, symphony and perfect co-ordination of the body and the mind. So even though you may arch your back into a perfect bow or split at an exact 180 degrees or balance and even bounce perfectly on the crown of your head, you may still be doing nothing more than gymnastics. Where lies the difference then? This may best be answered by the practitioner himself who concentrates on not only the flex of each muscle but also on the flow of consciousness. The realization of this Consciousness through your body is Yoga.

Yoga is one of the six systems of orthodox Hindu philosophy. Furthermore, it is of six types – *Bhakti Yoga* (or devotion to Lord Krishna which is truly manifest in the popular ISKCON Movement); *Jnana Yoga* (or realization through intellectual pursuits); *Karma Yoga* (or salvation through action); *Kundalini Yoga* (or practice of intense meditation);*Tantra Yoga* (or mystical, ritualistic and to an extent magical practices); finally *Hatha Yoga* (or physical practices). *Hatha Yoga*, due to its physiotherapeutic and hence curative nature is lately becoming more popular than any other form of Yoga.

In order to facilitate a healthy and balanced practice of Yoga Lord Mahadev, the supposed Founder of Yoga, laid down the eight-fold path or Ashtanga Yoga. Yama and Niyama are the ethical and moral disciplinary codes that gear you for the next step – Asanas. Healthy body leads to a healthy mind. So training and purification of the body is followed by the regulation of Breath-Pranayama. The control of Senses (Pratyahara); and concentration (Dharana) are followed by meditation or Dhyana. Yoga also means uniting with the one you seek or communion of Individual Self and Godhead.

Yoga is about the right attitude, perspective and the path you choose. Lord Krishna was a great Karma Yogi. In the modern era, another mortal amongst us who made himself immortal through Karma Yoga is Mahatma Gandhi. In our day-to-day lives, we find people working day in and day out to reach a goal with honest perseverance, dedication and bare minimum accolades. These are another set of Yogis. Yoga has as its aim - Perfection. Hence 'Yoga karmasu kaushalam' which maybe translated as Yoga inspires you to be the best version of yourself in any job you do.

As B.K.S. Iyengar rightly puts it - 'My Body is my temple; and asanas are my prayers'.

## Easy Yoga workout for kids

Teaching yoga to children can be fun. It is much too difficult to make yoga easy for kids after you have taught yoga to adults though. Adult training incorporates a formatted style of yoga training and teaching. But for kids you need to make a yoga session not just interesting and fun but also easy and energetic at the same time. You have to make it seem like an exercise or a 'play' without making it seem like a gymnastic 'performance' or a hard-core yogic posture. You have to make children love yoga so that they take to it as a lovable activity or a game. This alone has kept me glued to the art of training among children.

It's interesting when I was teaching a class of about five kids, I had a mixed bag with one obese child, one very thin, one flabby child and the other two flexible, intelligent, quick-learners and craving for more. It was a pleasure to teach the intelligent ones of course. But the obese child could not bend her leg fully in the Warrior Pose or could not touch her feet in the Plough pose or could not touch her toes in the Pashchimottana Asana. It became important that I let her do as much as she could without pushing for more and infact had to tell her to relax so that she stop feeling guilty about not being able to deliver more than others or more than she ought to. That's the worst feeling as a student. The worst feeling one can develop towards something new you are going out there to learn. Its about how much her body would allow. Does that mean I bifurcate the class into very intelligent and less intelligent class? Well, no. I just keep decomplicate things for them.

Simply, I did teach the more intelligent ones separately while playing with them. So they even managed to do the Yoganidra Asana and the Hanuman Asana (the split) with ease. Making yoga fun is important, irrespective of what the background of the student is.

For kids, introducing them to different poses itself is such an important job done. A perfect day for youngsters would mean a workout consisting of the following poses:

- Mountain Pose (Tadasana)
- Chair Pose (Utkatasana)
- Tree Pose (Vrikshasana)
- Eagle Pose (Garudasana)
- Forward Bend (Uttanasana)
- Downward Facing Dog (Adho Mukha Svanasana)

Among sitting postures the following basic asanas would be good

- Torso Stretch (Bharadvajasana)
- One-legged Forward Bend (Eik Pada Paschimottanasana)
- Half Bound Lotus (Ardha Baddha Pada Paschimottanasana)
- Hero Pose (Virasana)
- Seated Mountain Pose (Parvatasana)
- Cow Faced Pose (Gomukhasana)
- Half Lord of the Fishes (Ardha Matsyendrasana)

Finally daily practice of the Shoulder Stand (Sarvanga Asana) is good enough to end with. Medically, children need to stay fit. Physical, mental and social well-being of a child is important and yoga helps keep this balance as the performance of these asanas keeps the biological changes in balance within a body. The sooner, the better!

## Yoga for Menstruation

Women go through major changes in three stages of their lives- puberty, pregnancy and menopause. During a menstrual cycle, one needs to get used to a lot of hormonal changes within the body. The following combos can prove to be useful.

A good combination of poses to get rid of pre-menstrual tension is as follows:

## Combo 1

- Baddhakona Asana
- Supta Baddhakona Asana
- Supta Vira Asana
- Matsya Asana
- Sirsa Asana (against the wall for beginners)
- Sarvanga Asana
- Viparita Danda Asana
- Savasana

But if you probably need to take a pill for abdominal cramps, then stop. While your menstrual cycle is on, there are some wonderful poses you can do that can help you get rid of the pain and the mental stress. So a regular workout at this time can incorporate the following poses:

## Combo 2

- Utthita Trikona Asana
- Virabhadra Asana I
- Virabhadra Asana II

- Ardhachandra Asana
- Prasarita Padottana Asana
- Baddhakona Asana
- Upavishtakona Asana
- Janusirsa Asana
- Vir Asana with your head forward
- Setubandha Asana on 2 bolsters placed across each other

In each of these asanas focus is on the abdominal muscles and how these can be relaxed. Over-exertion should be avoided. In case of menstrual disorders, asanas should be done so that abdominal muscles and the organs have to be moved towards the spinal column as well as up towards the chest to avoid undue pressure on the uterus. If suffering from numbness, heaviness and aches, practitioner can do the following:

## Combo 3

- Utthita Parsvakona Asana
- Supta Baddhakona Asana
- Upavishtakona Asana
- Kurma Asana
- Mala Asana
- Vir Asana
- Supta Vir Asana

Dizziness during menstruation may be troublesome and the following asanas are beneficial for this:

## Combo 4

- Vir Asana

- Janu Sirsa Asana
- Ardha Baddha Padma Paschimottana Asana
- Trianga Mukhaikapada Paschimottana Asana
- Marichya Asana I

Incase of a profuse discharge, cramp or menorrhagia (excessive bleeding during menstrual periods), the workout should include the poses given here:

## Combo 5

- Baddhakona Asana
- Supta Baddhakona Asana
- Upavishtakona Asana
- Vir Asana
- Supta Vira Asana
- Paschimottana Asana
- Kurma Asana
- Urdhva Prasarita Pada Asana (with feet and legs supported by a wall)
- Adhomukhasvana Asana
- Padangushtha Asana (with a concave back)
- Prasarita Padottana Asana (with a concave back)

All combos given above aim at relieving the stress arising due to menstrual cycles, psychosomatic disorders and mental stress that can easily be handled if one performs these poses religiously. All asanas must be practised regularly even when menses are not on. It is only then that pain in the stomach, waist and back, heaviness in the abdomen and burning sensation may be gotten rid of. More than the physical anatomy, it is the mood disorders that need to be kept in check during this time, especially among younger women.

## Yoga as a Pre-Natal workout

Pregnancy is an important milestone in a woman's life. At this stage it is equally important for the mother to stay healthy, physically and mentally, as that affects the well-being of the child to be born. It is, therefore, important for the woman to continue to exercise, without over-exerting. This way the uterus is kept strong to function more efficiently so that delivery can be normal.

Yoga poses are truly beneficial against miscarriages. These are also good as a measure against failure to conceive due to defects of the ovaries, glands or fallopian tubes. Ideally, yoga poses must be done even prior to conception if one is to take pre-natal exercise seriously.

In order to prevent miscarriages, following asanas must be done so that conception can take place and hormonal balance can be achieved:

- Sirsa Asana (against the wall for beginners)
- Sarvanaga Asana
- Setubandha Asana
- Janusirsa Asana with variations

During the first three months, mother needs to be careful keeping her blood pressure normal. Yoga poses, however, strengthen pelvic muscles and the pelvic region improving blood circulation around the area. Reproductive system is strengthened, spine strong making the period of confinement bearable. The following poses in the first three months of pregnancy are very good for the mother and the baby:

- Parvata Asana

- Supta Vira Asana
- Upavishtakona Asana
- Baddhakona Asana
- Supta Padangushtha Asana

Light asanas which bring lightness to the abdomen and pelvis must be done on a regular basis. These provide nourishment to the uterus. When breathing becomes heavy, however, these should be stopped. Good asanas to be done at this stage are:

- Janusirsa Asana
- Baddhakona Asana
- Supta Baddhakona Asana
- Upavishtakona Asana
- Bharadwaja Asana
- Vir Asana and cycle
- Supta Vir Asana
- Parvata Asana
- Sava Asana

In the early stages of pregnancy morning sickness, dullness and weakness may appear. There may even be discharges or pains in the pelvic region, swelling or numbness in the feet, backache, constipation, variation in blood pressure, headache, dizziness and blurred vision. Asanas are useful in all such instances.

Normal Pranayama and breathing is also recommended for all months until delivery. As regards meditation, Sanmukhi Mudra, Sava Asana and Dhyana is to be done until the end of pregnancy. These are good not only for the physical well-being but also for making the mind strong and healthy. Some forms of basic Pranayama are:

- Ujjayi Pranayama I
- Viloma Pranayama I
- Viloma Pranayama II

It is said that the breathing exercises are good for development of the child in the womb and the easy expulsion of the child at the time of delivery. Practice of Pranayama even minimizes spasms and strains during labour and makes delivery easy for the mother as she knows the right type of relaxation. Yoga is just an easy assurance that you will sail through your pregnancy, taking good care of yourself and your baby.

## Yoga as a Post-Natal Workout

Yoga is a great workout for a mother post-delivery. But yoga is not just a physical session of heavy poses. It is meant to be a 'union' of body, mind and soul. As the Sanskrit word 'Yuj' means unity of mind and body, yoga aims at achieving harmony within the body. What better way to rejuvenate after delivery than yoga, where you actually feel every muscle and nerve come back to its usual shape while performing every asana.

In the first month after delivery, women are recommended full and complete rest, simply performing Pranayama. Fifteen days of rest can be followed by:

- Sava Asana
- Ujjayi Pranayama
- Viloma Pranayama

Second month onwards a good workout for an average practitioner is here:

| Week 1 | Week 2 | Week 3 | Week 4 |
|---|---|---|---|
| Vriksha Asana | Virabhadra Asana II | Paschimottana | Parvata Asana |
| Utthita Trikona Utthita Parsvakona | Uttana Asana | Janusirsa Asana Maha Mudra | Nava Asana Setu Bandha |
| | | | Bharadwaja Asana I Sarvanga (5 seconds) Hala (5 seconds) Paschimottana |

In the third month health of the mother should improve. Yoga should not end up in fatigues but should work to soothe and calm the muscles of the abdomen. If this is achieved, practitioner will feel at rest. As the mother gains original shape by the third month, practice of most asanas may be resumed.

Practice of asanas at this time tones the nervous system, strengthens the spinal column, stomach and abdomen. The waist can remain slim and non-flabby due to constant practice. If the delivery has been abnormal or there has been a Caesarean operation, one cannot do the poses until the wound heals. This may take upto two months. After that one can do Sava Asana, Ujjayi Pranayama I and Viloma Pranayama I.

Certain poses can be done after the initial months of rest and healing:

- Sarvanga Asana
- Hala Asana
- Setubandha Asana
- Parvata Asana
- Janusirsa Asana
- Maha Mudra
- Sava Asana

Few more poses which could add to strengthen abdominal and lumbar muscles as a post-natal workout are:

- Urdhva Prasarita Pada Asana
- Nava Asana
- Jathara Parivartana Asana

- Urdhvamukha Paschimottana Asana II
- Supta Padangushtha Asana
- Utthita Hasta Padangushtha Asana

If you think your stomach and abdomen have been worked upon and it is the back that needs to be taken care of, then some twisting poses could be good. In order to twist the spinal column and the trunk laterally these asanas will be good:

- Bharadwaja Asana I
- Bharadwaja Asana II
- Marichaya Asana III
- Ardha Matsyendra Asana
- Pasa Asana

If practiced religiously and with conscious breathing one can see wonders. A woman will feel back to her holistic health and rejuvenated vigor after pregnancy and child delivery. Post-natal care is as important for one as the baby care that is to follow in the years to come. Yoga simply prepares you for what is to come.

## Yoga for Menopause

Menopause can bring a lot of changes in women-hot flushes, high blood pressure, heaviness in the breasts, headaches, insomnia, obesity. At this time when women go through physiological and metabolic changes and also major changes in their psychological and emotional state, it is important for them to learn to manage their physical and mental stability. Some yoga poses can help you do just that.

Some standing poses and dynamic poses to practise at this time are:

- Prasarita Padottana Asana
- Uttana Asana
- Adhomukhasvana Asana
- Janusirsa Asana
- Paschimottana Asana
- Supta Vira Asana
- Matsya Asana

Menopause can lead to emotional disturbance, loss of balance and poise resulting in short temper, jealousy, depression, fear and anxiety. One may even feel a dismal loss of womanhood and a sudden feel of angst and deprivation. Yoga can help feel a sense of adjustment. Inverted poses and Pranayama that can help in this feeling of balance and equanimity are :

- Sirsa Asana
- Sarvanga Asana
- Hala Asana
- Setubandha Asana
- Dwipada Viparita Dandasana

- Ujjayi Pranayama I
- Viloma Pranayama

In this state, the endocrine system needs working upon and for that the following poses are beneficial:

- Upavishtakona Asana in Sirsa Asana (against the wall)
- Baddhakona Asana in Sirsa Asana (against the wall)
- Urdhva Padma Asana in Sirsa Asana (against the wall)
- Pinda Asana in Sirsa Asana (against the wall)
- Karnapida Asana
- Suptakona Asana
- Parsva Hala Asana
- Variations in Sarvanga Asana

Relaxation of the body and mind are most crucial at this stage for the woman. In order to help one realize this, these poses could prove to be useful:

- Parsvottana Asana
- Prasarita Padottana Asana
- Padangushtha Asana
- Uttana Asana
- Adhomukhasvana Asana
- Janusirsa Asana
- Ardha baddha Padma paschimottana Asana
- Trianga Mukhaikapada Paschimottana Asana
- Marichya Asana I
- Paschimottana Asana

Backbends assist majorly in stretching the spinal column making the blood circulate more freely. Opening of the chest here energises the lungs and rejuvenates the body and mind. This workout is good after one has gotten over the menopausal situation and wants to resume yoga. In order to get back to a regular yoga routine, it is a good workout:

- Ustra Asana
- Urdhvamukhasvana Asana
- Dhanur Asana
- Urdhvadhanura Asana
- Dwipada Viparita Danda Asana

These asanas are useful for an anxious state of mind and also for depression. The backbends prescribed above are very productive for getting rid of tension and resting the nervous system. It helps in keeping the body supple, improving respiration and relieving pain in the sacrum and the coccyx. These poses also remove dullness and laziness essential for pulling women out of their sluggish and irritable mental state of mind in menopause. Practise of yoga recommended above soothes the mind and strengthens one emotionally.

## Yoga with Props

As Yoga guru B.K.S. Iyengar puts it- 'The greatest form of communication is one that takes place within the body. That alone is the highest form of ethics.' The million-dollar question is- how to sustain that ethical communication? How to keep this communication alive so that the body, mind and soul all three work together as a whole. Different stages of yoga are simply the steps towards achieving this ideal level of oneness of body and spirit. When a practitioner cannot achieve the desired results in Yoga independently, we try to help a student do that with the help of yoga props such as the yoga block and the yoga strap.

## How To Use A Yoga Block: Use 1

So how to get started with yoga props. Let's start with the use of a yoga block. In a simple standing pose, if it is the hands you would like to work upon, then stand straight in Tada Asana or the Mountain Pose. Stretch out your arms placing the yoga block between your wrists holding the yoga block with the wrists. Slowly stretch your arms overhead and stay in this pose for a couple of minutes. This does wonder for your hands and your nerves around the palms. It is great if you sit for long hours in your office on a computer at your keyboard.

## How To Use A Yoga Block: Use 2

Another good use of the yoga block is again to strengthen the wrists. Stretch out your arms against the wall so that your fingers are placed on the floor. Place the yoga block between your forefingers and thumbs and stretch your legs out into the Dog Pose or Adhomukhasvana Asana.

## How To Use A Yoga Block: Use 3

A yoga block can also be used to straighten out your backbone, rather tailbone when you go up in the Bridge Pose or the Setubandha Asana. Lie down on a mat. Raise your butt off the floor to place the yoga block, vertically up, under your tailbone. Bend your legs at the knees. Adjust the yoga block. Stretch out your legs. Stretch your arms by the side.

## How ToUse A Yoga Strap: Use 1

If the yoga block can have these benefits for hands and tailbone, the yoga strap can be good for opening up the pelvis and for various other uses, too. First of all, sit in the Cobbler Pose or Baddhakona Asana. Increase the loop end of the yoga strap and take it over your head and tighten it around your waist and feet together. Pull the other end of the yoga strap on the right side. So that the pelvis opens, knees are pushed further down to the floor and feet are pulled closer to the body.

## How To Use A Yoga Strap: Use 2

The yoga strap is also used to do the Supta Padangustha Asana where the yoga strap is used to pull the toes closer to the torso. A good stretch of a leg can be achieved with the help of the yoga strap which is looped around the opposite raised toe.

## Yoga and Lifestyle

Yoga works like an elixir in today's sedentary lifestyle. In a fast-paced technological age, yoga alone has the power to heal, internally and externally, holistically and at a micro-level. All you need is the right trainer, guru and healer. So how can you start off feeling better if you are working twenty hours a day, six days of the week and 11 months in a year. Here's a lowdown on getting your biological clock ticking once again:

**Technological fast:** If you have that one day to rejuvenate take a break from all the gadgets and the gizmos around you. Let your body breathe easy without having to receive a phone-call, write an email, browse the net or even access your Facebook account. In short, keep a fast the modern way- switching your tech-world off. No to the tech-world (including the television or the radio or MP3) helps you give space to yourself as a person and human-being.

**Maun:** Maun Vrat or maintaining silence for twenty-four hours replenished you with oodles of energy, revitalizes your nerves, soothens your mind and rejuvenates you for a month. By keeping the maun vrat the implication is on not even talking to your little daughter or son, your loving wife or even your revered aunt or grandmother. Maintain complete silence without a hum or a sound and notice the wonders it will have on your biological system.

**Meditation:** Here you sit in a quiet corner of your room and fold your palms in a mudra or a pose; and meditate on your breath, navel or simply the emptiness of the mind. In this state, you need to close your eyes lightly without straining, release and relax the muscles of your face, eyes, ears and lips and focus on your mind or breath, whatever you choose.

**Breath:** Breath is the life-force of man. Empty your lungs out in a fresh environment-it could be your room. Breathe in after a full, heavy exhalation. Take about five to six such deep breaths with equally good exhalations. You should feel refreshed like a young bird.

**Exercise:** The most important part of revitalizing your organs is through great exercise. So what should be the starting-point and to what limits should you workout. Make sure you never overdo a workout routine. Yoga always focuses on relaxed exercising. This means simply doing as much as your body can without pushing the limits of your stretches and twists too far.

**Yama & Niyama:** Last but not the least is the dynamic sense of cleanliness, hygiene, truth, non-violence, self-control, non-accumulative, contentment, hard work and belief in yourself. The logic goes to- Positive In Positive Out just as a computer follows GIGO (Garbage In Garbage Out). A good assimilation, reading and practice of positive thought, word and deed helps you attain calmness and greater productivity at work.

So, try following these and supplement this daily routine with a fibre-induced organic diet, fruit and green vegetables and the whole regimen will leave you detoxified for the next lap of work. Next time you take time off from work, do not hesitate to follow this Yoga route or should I say, Yoga holiday. It may work wonders for you and your family.

## Connecting with Yogic Nature

It was a routine trip to the hills of Nainital. I went there with my husband and his friends for a regular getaway for three days but the experience was transformational. The connectivity and the proximity I felt with Nature was commendable.

This remote resort was by a flowing river at the base of a hill that stood towering above the rooms. Each room had glass windows that overlooked the running stream and the gurgling sound of it overpowered every other sound in the vicinity, even our own voices when we spoke.

As my friends and husband decided to take a walk in the woods, I decided to stay back and go the de-stress zone to do yoga. It is as though my body automatically flowed with the surrounding greens and the brook.

### Short yoga workout

It began with what may be called a short yoga warming up with the *Surya Namaskar* cycle. I lifted my arms straight up, bent down with the torso stretch almost touching my head to the knees, jumped to the dog pose to twitch to straighten my ribs with the crown of the head touching the floor, jumped again into what is normally called a 'push-up', then the dog pose II with head facing the thatched roof, repeated the same *asanas* backwards and finally stood upto do a *Namaste.* I repeated this 30 times.

Now it was time for some twisting poses to massage the spine. I started with *Bharadwaj asana* to the left and the right. I followed this with an *asana* which does wonders for diabetes- *Ardhamatsyendra asana*. I then twisted and straightened up into *Marichya asana* I, II and III.

I had to do the backbends, something that totally energizes me. I went on with the *Urdhvadhanur asana,* the shoulder stand and the bridge pose.

## Intensive meditation

Now it was time to soak in some good healthy air and I began inhaling and breathing deeply. I did some *Nadi Shodhana Pranayama* and began meditating. I finally ended with the chanting of *Om.*

As I continued to dabble with a few more stretches and chants, it was mesmerizing to see the rain on the roof and around me. The wetness all over made it seem a lot more surreal and beautiful.

While I got ready to walk away from the yoga zone rejuvenated I saw my friends walk in all sweaty and grimy and panting. They had had a hard day out with an uphill trek while I enjoyed turning inward to the soul and the body.

It was a wonderful connect with Nature !

# Section VI

# YOGA AND PHILOSOPHY

## Reiki and Yoga

Reiki is an art and a science developed by Japanese master Dr. Masako Usui. It is the science of focussing and meditating on different chakras of the body. Hence like yoga the idea is to focus on a body part and heal it internally by meditating upon it and applying various Japanese symbols on each body chakra to cleanse it.

There are several Japanese symbols used in Reiki, some of which have been discussed in detail here:

Cho-ku-re

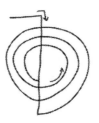

It is also called the Shakti symbol and is used on the seven chakras of the body in order to energize them. This symbol is used to instil energy and strength to the body. In order to purify something, too, the cho-ku-re symbol is used on all seven chakras.

Se-he-ki

This symbol is also called the mental symbol and is used to distress the mind, energize the mental organs and the brain and also to remove mental fatigue, etc. Emotional stress, fear, anger, resentment, negative thoughts are all controlled and quelled by the use of this symbol on the different chakras of the body.

Haun-sha-je-sho-nain

本
右
正
分
心

This symbol is also called the bridge symbol. It is used to ward off any evil or bad omen and is used on people sitting in a remote distance as well. It is used to control situations and anxieties and fears of the mind as well.

Similarly there are more symbols used under Karuna Reiki which is one of the advanced stages of Reiki practice. Two of those are discussed here:

Shanti

Shanti symbol is used to give peace to an individual and the world. This helps establish a balance between present, past and future.

Hosanna

This symbol helps remove obstacles and denotes independence. It is applied on all the chakras and can be used to heal people sitting in a remote corner of the world.

Reiki is hence about aura cleaning and healing the body from within.

## Hatha Yoga Pradipika

Yoga is called the most practical form of physical exercise and practice among all forms of exercises. In this a yogi truly experiences the benefits of Raja Yoga. The mantra is:

Yukvay savita devanswaryato ghiya divam

Brihajjyotiha karishyatah savita prasuvati taan (Yajur veda, 11, [3])

This means that with full devotion and faith whoever practices yoga with the aim of removing ignorance and negativities and achieving the Paramatma, towards that devotee the Parameshwar (Savita Dev) will be kind and will be blessed with Rithambara Pragya and this devotee will be in good health and spirit. Such a devotee will be full of Brihajjyoti-Paramjyoti and with Tatvagyan and Paramatmagyan.

Hatha yoga is a way of mastering the practice of the breath or Prana-Sadhana. Th creators of Hatha Yoga Pradipika made sure it contains verses related to basic tenets of Yoga and deals with the practical aspects of Raja Yoga. According to Sage Patanjali, the foremost proponents of Yoga said Yogashcritivrittinirodhaha or yoga works to get rid of all imbalances in body, mind and spirit. This constancy and control within the body is yoga. Ha implies Prana and Tha means balance. The right balance of Prana and Mann is Hatha Yoga. Through Hatha Yoga the body can get rid of all the ailments, mind and Mann become free of irregularities, heart rate gets stabilized and the vicissitudes of the Mind are gotten rid of. This way the yogi is always ready to perform her practice or sadhana. The practitioner thus becomes so energized that she can even look beyond death which is called Kalavanchan.

Hatha Yoga Pradipika says that here knowledge was transferred through Goddes Parvati who got this knowledge from Lord Shiva. It is through the hearing-memory-retention that this knowledge is passed on through the sages by Goddess Parvati. The meaning of Yoga is harmony of Jivatama and Paramatma. This knowledge is attained through good intent or shraddha which has been explained in this shloka of The Gita:

Shraddhavanlabhatey gyanam tatparah saiyantendriyaha (Gita, 4, [39])

The one who has full faith achieves full knowledge of Hatha Yoga and accomplishes the intricacies of Raja Yoga, too.

In Hatha Yoga an effort is made to get full control of Asana, Pranayama, Pratyahara, Dharana, Dhyana and Samadhi. Along with this Kundalini, Mudrabandha, Khatachakrabhedana and Nadanusandhan are also practised. Although yoga basically consists of eight steps or Ashtanga Yoga- yama, niyama, asana, pranayama, pratyahara, dharana, dhayana and Samadhi, here in Hatha Yoga, the six steps are given prominence- Pranayama onwards. A hatha Yoga practitioner must feel that whatever is in the Universe is also inside him or her. The inner knowledge and practice is given utmost importance in Hatha Yoga. Hatha Yoga Pradipika has been divided into four sermons.

**Sermon One (Asana)**

Pranamya shrigurum natham swatmaramein yogina

Kewalam rajayogay hathavidyopadishyatey [2]

Bow to your Guru with full respect and faith and for the fulfilment of Raja Yoga Yogi Swatmaram has given this sermon.

Asheshatapataptanam samshrayamathohathah
Asheshayogayuktanamadharkamatho hathah [10]

In this world all those who believe in penance and hard work, for them the goal is Hatha Yoga. For all yogis Hatha Yoga is the only solution.

Atyaharah prayasashcha prajalpo niyamgrahaha
Janasangashcha laulyam cha khadbhiryogo vinashyati [15]

Excessive food, labour, speech, socializing and lack of focus destroy yoga. These are the main obstacles to a good yoga practice.

Utsahaat sahasadhaiyartatvagyanaachcha nishchayat
Janasangaparityagatkhadbhiryogaha prasidhyyati [16]

Enthusiasm, patience, tatvagyan, determination and focussing on the self are main attributes of a successful yoga practice or sadhana.

Ahimsa satmasteyam brahmacharyakshama dhritiha
Dayarjavam mitaharaha shaucham chaiva yama dasha [17]

Tapah santosh aastikyam danameeshwarapooanam
Siddhantavaakyashravanam hrimati cha tapohutam
Niyama dasha samprokta yogashastravisharadaiha [18]

Non-violence, truth, asteya, brahmacharya, forgiveness, dhriti, kindness, simplicity, eating balanced amount of food, cleanliness of body are the ten disciplines of yama. Penance, contentment, belief in God, worshipping God, mati, tap and hawan are the ten disciplines of Niyama.

Hathasya prathamangatwadasanam poorvamuchyate
Kuryatatadasanam sthairyamarogyam changalaghawam [19]

Asana is the first step of Hatha Yoga. Therefore this step has to be mastered first. Asanas must be practiced which enhances stability, freedom from disease and increases body agility.

A few asanas mentioned in Hatha Yoga Pradipika are mentioned here with their benefits:

Swastika Asana

This is useful for Raja Yoga sadhana. This is also called sukha asana or simple cross-legged pose. In this asana the mind is made one and is useful in practicing pranayama. It is good for the spine and for sadhana. Those suffering from a lower back problem or from sciatica must not sit in this posture.

Gomukha Asana

This is good for the nerves and vessels within the body. This is also beneficial for the stomach, intestines and indigestion. It cures one of kidney problems, sciatica and even diabetes. It also cures one of any backaches.

Virasana

This is beneficial for meditating and practicing dhyana.

Kurmasana

The most important benefit is that it stabilizes the mind. It cures stomach liver and pancreas ailments. It is also good for kidney, hernia, piles, diabetes and obesity.

Uttana kurmasana

This asana brings flexibility to the body and energizes and rejuvenates all the nerves and Nadis. Stomach ailments are cured and heart becomes stronger. The body stays fit.

Aakarshan dhanurasana

This asana makes arms, chest and neck very strong. The body becomes more flexible; physical and emotional strength is increased; stomach is strengthened, body fat is lost and any body pain is gotten rid of.

Matsyendrasana

While doing this asana one must keep in mind that while twisting and doing Rechaka Pranayama, one has to exhale, and inhale after completely sitting in the pose facing the front. This asana is beneficial for all stomach ailments and intestinal disorders. It is good for the spine and the backbone, increases blood flow, improves digestion and cures diabetes. Headache and backaches are also soothened.

Pashchimottanasana

During this asana the yogi must put her dhyana in Swadhishthana chakra and all the attention must be on the body, spirit, mind, stomach, back, and the muscles of the back and the stomach. Digestion is improved through this asana, the nerves and veins and Nadis are cleaned. It treats obesity, cures diabetes and increases will power and spiritual power.

Yuva vridhhotivriddho va vyadhito durbalopiva
Abhyasatsiddhimapnoti sarvayogeshvatandritaha [66]

The practitioner may be a young, old or very old or diseased and weak person yoga and its practice makes one active and strong.

## Sermon Two (Pranayama)

Chale vaatey chalam chittam nishchaley nishchalam bhaveit
Yogi sthandutvamaapnoti tato vayum nirodhayteit [2]

The mind cannot be still if the Prana is not still it will remain in a constant state of flux. Once the Prana is constant, mind also becomes stable and focussed and the yogi becomes stable, too. The Prana must be retained in the body for a while (which is also called kumbhaka).

Yavad vayuh sthito dehey tavajjevanmuchyate
Maranam tasya nishkrantistato vayum nirodhayeit [3]

So long as the air is still within the body, there is life. The moment Prana exits the body, there is no life and the body is dead. Therefore an effort must be made to clean that Prana which is called Pranayama.

Pratarmadhyamdiney sayamardharatrey cha kumbhakaan
Shanairasheetiparyantam chaturvaram samabhyaseit [11]

A yogi must practice Pranayam four times a day- morning, afternoon, evening and night. Each time 80-80 Kumbhakas (breath retention) must be performed.

Pranayamein yuktein sarvarogakshayo bhaveit
Ayuktabhyasyogein sarvarogsamudbhavah [16]

If Pranayama is practiced with proper discipline and stepwise, all diseases are destroyed within the body. If proper steps are not followed, then problems may arise while practicing Pranayama.

Medah shleshamadhikaha poorva khat karmani samachareit
Anyastu nachareitanidoshanam samabhavatah [21]

If a yogi has too much fat and disease, she must practice six steps Khatkarma (dhauti, basti, neti, trataka, nauli, kapalabhati) first. The body is cleansed. Those who have the balance must not do this.

Kasashvasapleehakushtham kafarogashcha vinshatiha
Dhautikarmaprabhavein prayantyeva cha sanshaya [25]

Due to Dhauti, pancreas and spleen and twenty other types of diseases get cured.

Nabhidadhnajaley payau nyastanalotkatasana
Adharaakunchanam kuryat kshaalanam vastikarma tat [26]

The little finger has to be inserted into the anus after being seated in a couched position on the floor. Water must be entered into the anal cavity and cleansed. This is basti.

Kapalshodhinichaiv divyadrishtipradayani
Jatrurdhvajatarogaugham netirashu nihanti cha [30]

9 inches of a thickish tube is smoothened and is entered through the nose and brought out from the mouth. This is neti. Jal-neti is when water is poured through one nostril and comes out from the other nostril. This cleanses the nasal cavity.

Nirikshennishchaladdasha sookshmalakshyam samahitaha
Ashrusampatparyantamachaiyastratakam smritam [31]

Mochanam netraroganam tandradeenam kapatakam
Yatnatastratakam gopyam yatha hatakpetakam [32]

While focussing one has to look sharply at one point for a
long time until the eyes start watering. This is tratak. This
is beneficial for all eye problems. If one practices tartak
regularly it clears the mind and the eyes. After closing one's
eyes, if you focus your sight inward between the eyebrows,
on the heart or a the base of the stomach, it is inner trataka.

Amandavartavegein tundam savyapasavyatah
Natanso bhramyedesha nauliha sidhaiha prashasyate
Mandagnisandeepanpachanadi
Sandhapikanandakari sadaiv
Asheishadoshamayashoshani cha
Hathakriyamauliriyam cha nauliha [34]

One is supposed to do Nali Kriya which cleanses the body,
stomach and cures flatulence. Bend forward with both the
shoulders bent foward. Put your hands on both your knees
and suck your stomach in towards the back. Move your
stomach from left to right and vice versa. This is also called
Lauliki kriya and is very beneficial for stomach ailments and
digestion.

Pranayamaireiv sarvey prashushyanti malaa iti
Acharyanam tu keshanchidanyat karma na sammatam [37]

A lot of sages believe that all ailments and diseases can
be cured through Pranayam alone without having to do
Khatakarm or the six steps. They believe that all Nadis are
cleansed and purified through Pranayama.

Suryabhedanamunjaayee seetkari sheetali tatha
Bhastrika bhramari moorchha plaavinitshatakumbhakaaha [44]

There are eight types of Pranayama- Suryabhedan, ujjayi, seetkari, sheetali, bhastrika, moorchha and plaavini. According to Gheranda Samhita (5, 45) suryabheda, ujjayi, sheetali, bhastrika, bhramari, moorchha and kewali are eight kinds of kumbhaka or forms of breath retention in the body.

**Sermon Three (Mudras)**

Sashailvandhatreenam yathadharohinayakaha
Sarvesham yogatantranam tathadharo hi kundali [1]

Just as the base of Earth, full of forests and mountains, is Shesha (King of serpents), the base of all Yogic practices is raining the Kundalini. Yoga means Asana, pranayama, pratyahara, dharana, dhyana, Samadhi, mudra-bandha and other such sadhanas. If Kundalini cannot be raised then most of this yoga is without any meaning.

Sputa guruprasadein yada jagarti kundali
Tada sarvani padmani bhidyantey granthayopi cha [2]

If by pleasing the Guru one's Kundalini is raised, all six chakras within the body and granthis (Brahma, Vishnu, Mahesh) are energized and pierced by energy.

All the chakras- muladhara chakra, swadhishthan chakra, manipoorak chakra, anahata chakra, vishuddhi chakra and agya chakra are pierced and brahma granthi passes through anahata chakra and one experiences ananda or happiness.

Padmooleinvamein yonim sampeedya dakshinam
Prasaritam padam kritva karabhyam dharayeid dridham [10]
Kanthey bandham samaropyam dharayeid vayumoordhwatah
Dandahataha sarpo dandakarah prajayatey [11]
Rijweebhoota tatha shaktiha kundali sahasa bhaveit
Tada sa maranavastha jayatey dwiputashraya [12]
Tataha shanaih shanairevam rechayannaiv vegatah
Iyam khalu mahamudra mahasiddhaiha pradarshita [13]
Mahakleshayadayo doshaha ksheeyantey maranadayah
Mahamudraam cha tenaiva vadanti vibudhottamaah [14]

This explains the posture of mahamudra by placing your feet under the reproductive organs and extending the right leg out. While practicing this the vision should be focussed between the eyebrows. Then one must practice moolabandha and jalandhar bandha slowly and retain breath while bending down on the right leg. This must be repeated on the other side. Kundalini is raised like this.

Mahabandhaha parobandho jaramaranashanaha
Prasadadasyabandhasya sadhayeit sarvavaanchhitam

This Bandha strengthens the body. The entire body gets purified and cleansed.

Bhruvorantargatam drishtim vidhaya sudridha sudheeha
Upavishyasaney vajrey nanopadravavarjitaha
Lambikordhwasthiteygartey rasanam viparitagam
Sanyojayeit prayatnein sudhakoopey vichakshanam
Mudraisha khechriprokta bhaktanamanurodhataha

The practitioner stabilizes the vision between the eyebrows, keeps the mind steady and still in vajrasana (couched on your knees and sitting on ankles). The tongue is rolled up towards the palate. This is called Khechri-Mudra and vyomachakara.

Moordhnaha shodashapatrapadmagalitam pranaddavaptam hatha
Doordhwasyo rasanam niyamya vivarey shaktim pagam chintayan
Utkallolkalajalam cha vimal dharamayam yaha pibey
Nnirvyadhiha sa mrinankomalvapuryogi chiram jeevati [51]

The one who looks up after twirling the tongue gets rid of all diseases. He attains Prana. Udarey pashchimam tanam nabheyrurdhwam cha karayeit
Uddiyano hyaso bandho mrityumaatangakesari [57]
Uddiyanam tu sahajam guruna kathitam sada
Abhyaseit satatam yastu vridhhopi tarunayatey [58]

The one who does Uddiyana Bandha by sucking in the stomach becomes as energized as the lion. This is the most natural posture. If an old man does it everyday, he feels energized like a young person and a youthful human being.

Parshinabhaagein sampeedya yonimakunchayedgudam
Apanamoordhwamakrishya moolabandhobhidheeyatey [61]
Adhogatimpanam va urdhwagam kurutey balat
Akunchanein tam prahurmoolabandham hi yoginaha [62]

Now the practitioner focuses on the reproductive organs and the anus and sucks in from that cavity into the stomach. This is Moolabandha. This way the air underneath is sucked into the body, this is proper moolabandha. It assists in raising the kundalini.

Kanthamakunchya hridaye sthapayechchibukam dridham
Bandho jalandharakhyoyam jaramrityuvinashakaha [70]
Badhnati hi shirajalmadhogami nabhojalam
Tato jalandharo bandhaha kanthadukhoghanshanaha [71]

Now at the throat one has to suck in the air around it and tighten the area around it. The chin must face down between the collar bones. This is Jalandhar Bandha. Once the tension is released, this is good for all throat ailments. The focus here is on Vishuddhi Chakra.

Urdhwanabheradhastaloroorghwa bhanuradhaha shashi
Karani viparitakhya guruvakyein labhayatey [79]

The posture in which the tongue and palate are towards the floor and the belly is facing upward is called Viparitakarni.

Upadesh hi mudranaan yo dattey sampradayikam
Sa eiv shriguruha swami sakshadeeshwar evam saha [129]

The person who delivers a traditional- guru-based practice, he or she is the true guru, swami and close to God's own nature.
Tasya vakyaparo bhootwa mudrabhyasey samahitaha
Animadigunaiha sardham labhatey kalavanchanam [130]

A yogi should practice the guru who has mastered asana, pranayama and mudra, etc. and tide over the fear of death.

## Sermon Four (Samadhi)

Namah shivay guruve nadabindukalatmaney
Niranjanpadam yaati nityam yatra parayanaha [1]

Due to Pranayama there is immense energy inside the body. Guru is like Lord Shiva and Lord Shiva is the guru. Due to obstacles that may arise in the process of yoga and overcoming those obstacles is a must. Therefore mangalacharan has to be organized.

Swavishaya samprayogey chittaswaroopanukar ivendriyanam pratyaharaha (yogadarshan, 2, 54)

In Gheranada Samhita it is said that an unstable mind must get stilled in objects or things which still the mind.

Deshabandhashchittasya dharana tatra pratyayaikatanatadhyanam (Yogadarshan, 3, 1-2)

Dharana and dhayana are parts of Samadhi and Samadhi is full of parts. Maharshi Patanjali has explained the different parts and qualities of Samadhi.

Sahajam swatmasamvittiha sainyamaha swaswanigrahaha Sopayam swaswavishrantiradwaitam paramam padam (sidhasidhantapadhati, 5, 30)

The true knowledge is the knowledge between Jivatma and Paramatma. Controlling your senses and focussing on atma is good control.

Vividhairasanaiha kumbhairvichitraiha karanairapi Prabaddhayam mahashaktau pranahashoonye praleeyatey [10]

With the practice of Matsyendra, siddha and swastika asana, kumbhaka pranayama and mudras immense energy is produced and prana gets assimilated in brahma.

Amaraya namastubhyam sopi kalastavyaya jitaha
Patitam vadaney yasya jagadeitachcharacharam [13]

O Immortal Yogi! I bow to you. The one who has won over death and the entire world is at your feet.

Chittey samatwapanney vaiyau brajati madhyamey
Tadamaroli vajroli sahajoli prajayatey [14]

Once the mind is stilled and prana enters sushumna Nadi, then amrauli, vijroli and sahajoli mudras are achieved.

Suryachandramasau dhattaha kalam ratrimdivatmakam
Bhoktro sushumna kalasya gyhyameitdudahyatam [17]

Only once the prana is brought into a constant beat, the mind is stilled and one has achieved victory. One the prana is in Ida and Pingla Nadis, mind wanders and true victory is achieved once prana enters Sushumna Nadi.

Manaha sthairyo sthiro vayusto binduha sthiro bhaveit
Bindusthairyat sada satvam pindasthairyam prajayatey [28]

Once the mind is stilled, Prana is stilled and once the Prana is stilled, body becomes clean, pure and strong and remains healthy for a long time.

Netranjanam samalokya atmarama nirikshayeit
Sa bhavechhambhavi mudra sarvatantreishu gopita

Shambhavem yo vijanati sa cha brahma na chanyatha
(Gheranda Samhita, 3, 64, 97)

Shambhavi Mudra is to focus one's attention between the eyebrows and stay there for a long time in that position. The one who knows Shambhavi Mudra is the ultimate victor.

Muktasaney sthito yogi mudra sandhaya shambhaveem
Shrinuyaddakshiney karney nadamanteasthamekadheeha [67]

Yogi must do shamabhavi mudra in siddhasana and hear from the right ear.

Manomattagajendrasya vishayodyanachaarinaha
Samarthoyam niyamaney ninadinishitankushaha [91]
Badhdham tu nadbandhein manaha santyaktachapalam
Prayati sutaram sthairyam chhinapakshaha khago yatha [92]

The mind is like an elephant who has been left to wander in the wild. Just as Nad is appropriate to still a wandering mind, the mind should not get carried away by material objects and should try and abandon material things. Then the mind is stilled like a bird is stilled without its feathers.

Sarvey hathalayayogapaya rajayogasya siddhaye
Rajayogasamaroodhaha purushaha kalavanchakaha

Asana, kumbhaka, pranayama, mudra-bandha are Hatha and nada, shambhavi mudra are laya. Both these are good for achieveing the stillness and calmness of the mind and achieving Raja Yoga. The one who achieves Raja Yoga can overcome death and make his life longer.

Khadyatey na cha kalein badhyatey na cha karmana
Sadhyatey na sa kenapi yogi yuktaha samadhina [108]
In Samadhi, a yogi does not fear being given death before
time. The Yogi is then not bound by shubha-ashubha
consequences of actions. Nor can such a yogi be cowered by
tantra-yantra-mantra or witchcraft or black magic.

Chittam na suptam no jagratsmritivismritivarjitam
Na chasmeiti nodeiti yasyasau mukta eiv saha [110]

The yogi who is beyond memory and loss, sleep and
awakened state, active and dull state, that yogi is free of any
vices and is completely without bondage.

Yavad dhyaney sahajsadrisham jayatey naiva tatwam
Tatwajgyanam vadati tadidam dambhamithyapralapaha
[114]

So long as Prana remain in Sushumna Nadi it is stilled.
Prolonged stay in such a state leads to atmagyana.

Aamkumbhamivambhastho jeeryamanaha sada ghataha
Yoganaleina sandahyam ghatashuddhim samachareit

Just as an earthen pot is baked so that water stays in it and
doesn't spill out, the body is constantly decaying. Yoga helps
rejuvenate and make the body strong enough and works
like a fire baking the body to keep it going clean, steady
and healthy.

## Chanting with Faith

Some Yogic chants which can do wonders for the body, mind and soul:

### Gayatri Mantra
Om Bhurbhuvaha Swaha Tatsaviturvarenyam
Bhargo devasya dheemahi
Dhiyo yo Naha Prachodayat

### Mahamrityunjaya Jaap
Om Trayambakam yajamahey sugandhim Pushtivardhanam
Urvarukmiv bandhanaat mrityormukshiya mamritaat

### Saka Gokkai Chant
Nam Myo Ho Renge Kyo

### Buddhist Chant
Om Maney Padmey Hom

Each chant must be done while sitting in Virasana or siddhasana or Swastika asana. Chants must be done for a minimum of five minutes and can go upto two or three hours. The chants are useful when one feels low, depressed, undermotivated, stressed and to gather renewed vigour and enthusiasm in life.

## Excerpts from the Bhagvad Gita

The Gita is a book of life. It trains one in day-to-day activities and enhances one's coping skills. Shrimadbhagvadgita here has many purposes and one of its major purpose is to show one the way for a healthy life in which one learns to manage various relationships with friends, family, peers and colleagues. Here are some main shlokas or Sanskrit verses to assist in such harmonious living:

Vasansi jeernani yatha vihaya
Navani grihanati naroparani
Tatha shareerani vihaya jeerna
Nyanyani sanyati navani dehi [2, 22]

Just as an individual discards old clothes and adorns fresh clothes, in the similar manner a spirit takes off old body of an individual and takes the form of a new body after death.

Nayanam chhindanti shastrani nayanam dahati pawakaha
Na chainam kledayantapo na shoshayati maarutaha [2. 23]

A spirit cannot be cut by a weapon, fire cannot douse it, water cannot dissolve it nor can it dry up due to wind. Such is the nature of the Spirit.

Karmanyewadhikarastey ma phaleshu kadachana
Ma karmaphalaheturbhurma te sangostwakarmani [2. 47]

You only have a right over the Karma or the deed that you perform, not in the fruits of your actions. Therefore you must not waste your energy in thinking about the results of your actions but at the same time you must have not ignore your actions.

Actions make your destiny eventually.

Yadyadacharati shreshtastattadevetaro janah
Sa yatpramanam kurutey lokastadanuvartatey [3, 21]

What a mature and accomplished person does is emulated by others. Whatever the accomplished person produces as proof is repeated by the others. That is the value of being accomplished in one's life.

Kama eisha krodha eisha rajogunasamudbhavaha
Mahashano mahapapma vidhyenamiha vairinama [3. 37]

Rajoguna is a quality in a person where if he gets angry it is the biggest vice and a sin. Anger is the greatest enemy.

Yada yada hi dharmasya glanirbhavati Bharata
Abhyuthanam adharmasya tadatmanam srijamyaham [4, 7]

O Bharat! Whenever there is the downfall of Dharma or Good and an increase in Evil, then I come back into Earth and take birth as a human-being. I make myself visible before the people of this planet.

Paritranaya sadhunaam vinashaya cha dushkritam
Dharmasansthapanarthaya sambhavami yugey yugey [4, 8]

In order to salvage the good persons, destroying the evil-doers, and re-establishing the good faith and order in the community, I come on this planet in every era and Age.

Yasya sarvey samarambhaaha kamsankalpavarjitaaha

Gyanagnidagdhakarmanam tamahuha panditam budhaaha [4, 19]

That whose knowledge of shastras or Hindu texts is without any desire but full of determination; that whose actions are immersed in knowledge that great person is called a Pandit or the one with Knowledge.

Yadrichhalabhasantushto dwandwateeto vimatsaraha
Samaha siddhavasidhhau cha kritwaapi na nibadhyatey [4, 22]

That person who is satisfied within himself or herself without having gotten anything, the one who has no room for jealousy, the one who has become beyond the daily joys and sorrows, such a person who stays calm and composed in achievement and accomplishment is a Karma Yogi to whom any Karma will not be binding. Such a person is free of bondage and has complete freedom.

Shreyandravyamayaadyagyangyan yagyaha parantap
Sarvam karmakhilam partha gyaney parisamaapyatey [4, 33]

O Arjun! Gyan yagya or sacrifice is more significant than the sacrifice of the waters. All the actions sublimate in the Knowledge of the Divine.

Na hi gyanein sadrisham pavitramiha vidyatey
Tatswayam yogasansidhhaha kaleinatmani vindati [4, 38]

In this world there is nothing that purifies one more than knowledge. A lot of this knowledge is obtained by one gradually.

Shraddhavanllabhate gyanam tatparaha sainyatendriyaha
Gyanam labhdwa paraam shantimchireinadhigachhati [4, 39]

The one who has attained victory over one's senses, and one full of faith and belief attain knowledge and through that knowledge attain oneness with God soon enough. Such is the power of Knowledge.

Gyeyaha sa nityasanyasi yon a dweshti na kankshati
Nirdwandwo hi mahabaho sukham bandhatpramuchyatey [5, 3]

O Arjun! That person who does not feel jealous or is not very ambitious, that Karma Yogi is full of actions and is a true Sanyasi; because a person free of bad faith and jealousy is freed of the worldly bondage.

Yogayukto vishuddhatma vijitatma jitendriyaha
Sarvabhootatmabhootatmaa kurvannapi na lipyatey [5, 7]

The one whose mind and spirit are in one's control, the one who is pure and has overcome the senses, the one for whom all living beings are the same and one, such a Karma Yogi performs action without getting entangled in her or his own actions. He or she is a true Yogi.

Bharhmanadhaya karmaani sanga vyaktwa karoti yaha
Lipyatey na sa papein padmapatramivambhasa [5, 10]

A person who performs actions by dedicating all his actions to the Divine, the one who performs actions without attachment, that person is like the lotus flower from water and is free of any sin. He or she is a pure human-being.

Na prahrishyetpriyam prapya nodwijetprapya chapriyam
Sthirabudhhirasammoodho brahmavid brahmani sthitaha
[5, 20]

That person who is not overjoyed after encountering the
good, and is not disturbed after facing hardships that person
is cool, calm and composed, is free of doubt and is one with
the Brahma- the God.
Shankoteehaiv yaha sodhum prakshareeravimokshanaat
Kamakrodhodbhavam vegam sa yuktaha sa sukhi narah [5, 23]

That practitioner who even before death is able to gain
complete control over one's anger-desire and anything born
out of both of these, that person alone is a true Yogi and is
happy in life.

Anashritaha karmaphalam karyam karma karoti yaha
Sa sanyasi cha yogi cha na niragnirna chakriyaha [6, 1]

That person who is not dependent on the results of his actions
and only performs his actions with a single-mindedness,
that person is a Sanyasi and a Yogi. That Sanyasi does not
sacrifice fire alone or does not give up action completely.

Yada hi nendriyartheshu na karmaswanushajjyate
Sarvasankalpasanyasi yogaroodhastadochyatey [6, 4]

At a time when a person is not indulging in the senses or the
worldly pleasures or does not get carried away by actions,
that time the sacrificing person is moving towards Yoga.

Uddharedaatmanatmanam natmanamavsaadayeit
Aatmaiv hyatmano bandhuratmaiv ripuratmanaha [6, 5]

One should use oneself and one's body to salvage oneself, and should not put oneself into bad habits; because one is one's own enemy and one's own friend alike. There is no better friend than yourself and no worse enemy than your own self.

Asanshayam mahabaho mano durnigraham chalam
Abhyasein tu kaunteiya vairagyein cha grihyatey [6, 35]

O the Powerful One! No doubt the mind is fleeting and runs hither and thither.and it is difficult to tame the mind. But O Arjuna, with practice and renunciation the mind can be controlled.

With these main verses, it may be said that Yoga is a balance of the body, mind and soul so that one attains complete harmony physically and spiritually. Yoga is hence a way of life and a certain control to be adopted by anybody who wants to attain peace, contentment and bliss along with good health.